To:

From:

PAGE PUBLISHING
Conneaut Lake, PA

First originally published by Page Publishing 2024

ISBN 979-8-89315-637-9 (pbk)
ISBN 979-8-89315-683-6 (hc)
ISBN 979-8-89315-658-4 (digital)

Printed in the United States of America

If I Could Be Mommy for One More Day

A GRANDMOTHER'S WISH

Michael Paladines

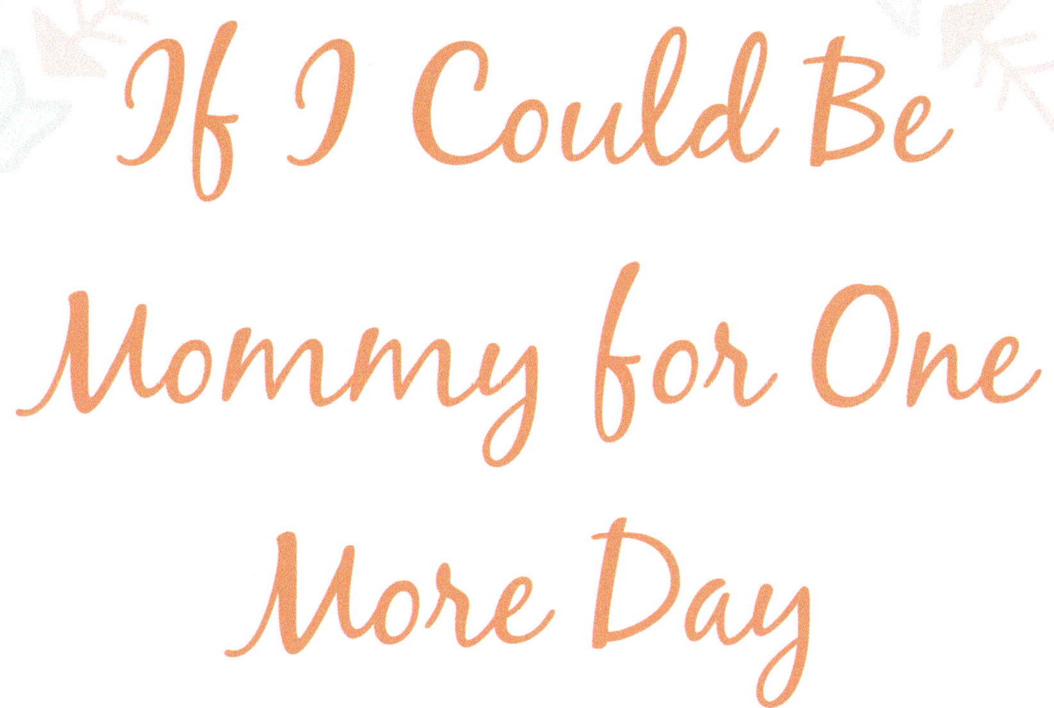

"To my wife Hope and children Michael, Cameron and Hayley.
Who have kept me grounded and shown me the true definition of joy."

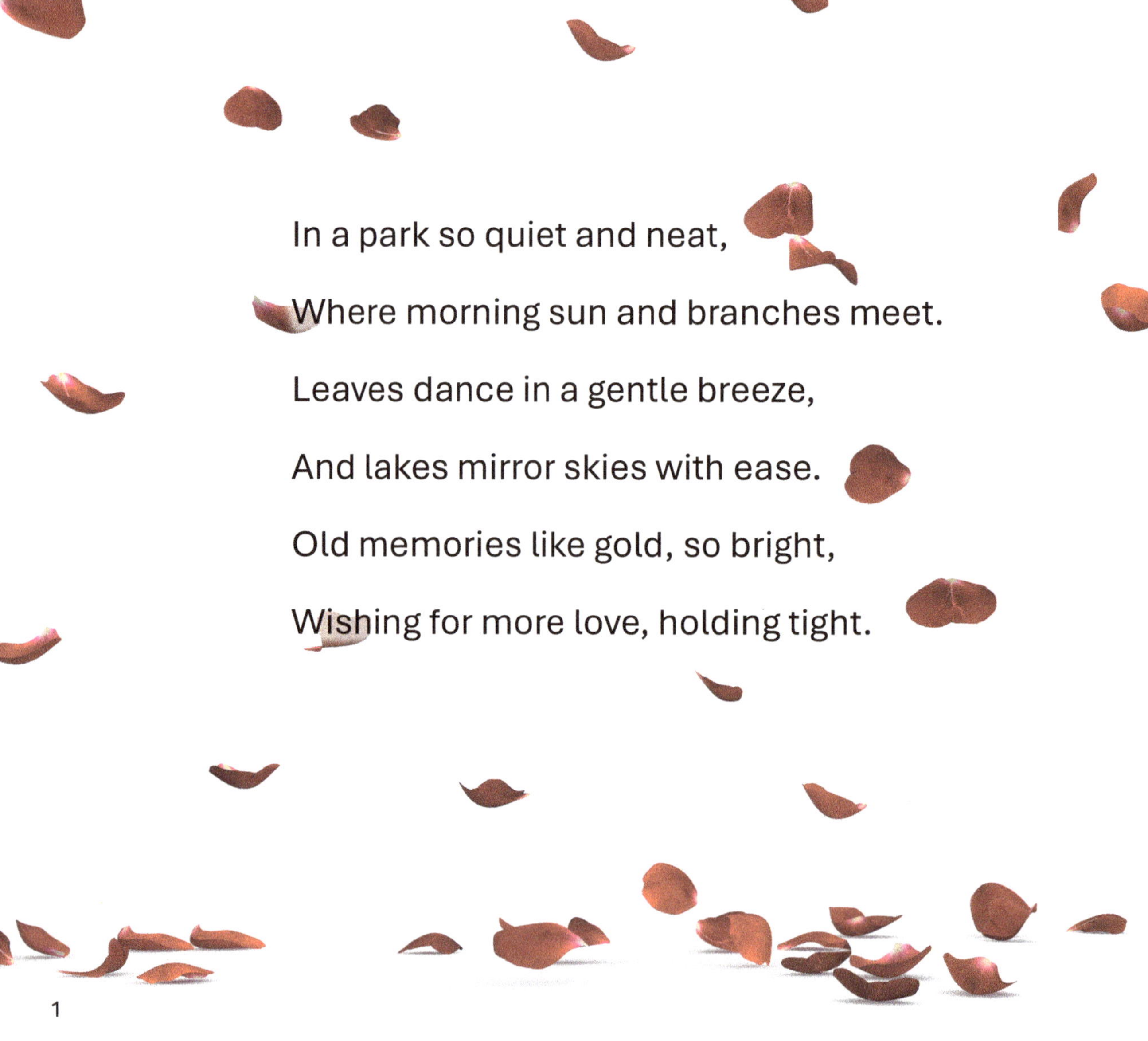

In a park so quiet and neat,

Where morning sun and branches meet.

Leaves dance in a gentle breeze,

And lakes mirror skies with ease.

Old memories like gold, so bright,

Wishing for more love, holding tight.

1

A light so bright, it hums and sings,

Turning wishes into magical things.

While in the barn, we laugh and play,

Adventures await, in bright of day.

My hand in your mane, so small and sweet,

Together, we're ready for every feat.

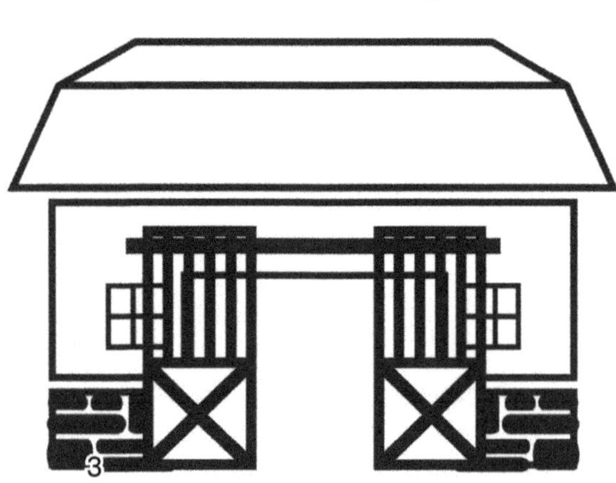

On the field under the sunny sky,

My boy runs fast, his spirits high.

With a cheer, he throws, the crowd roars loud,

His victory bright, makes me so proud.

"That's my boy!" I shout, full of glee,

In these moments, the magic of motherhood I see.

Up in the sky, so vast and blue,

A dream takes flight, so bold and true.

At nine, with eyes so wide and bright,

A pilot's visit, makes this a guiding light.

"Mama, look!" you point and say,

"Up there, I'll fly, so high, one day."

Sandy toes and salty air,

Beach adventures, without a care.

At eleven, you're strong and bold,

Protecting siblings, a sight to behold.

Laughter with the tide, a joyful ride,

In motherhood, my heart takes pride.

Halloween night, a parade in sight,

A little hero, shining so bright.

With a cape so bold, in the moon's soft light,

Candy buckets full, oh what a delight!

Eyes sparkling with joy, a blissful sight,

Childhood magic, glowing so bright.

Christmas dawn, with light so bright,

Gifts unwrap in morning's light.

Six little eyes, so wide with glee,

Beneath the tree, a family spree.

Warmth and love at every glance,

In these moments, memories dance.

13

14

Seventy years, a gentle breeze,

Memories like leaves in trees.

Preschool games, cheers so loud,

Cameras flashing, a joyful crowd.

Sun-kissed face, four years bold,

"Mommy, I won!" A story told.

First day of school, so vast and wide,

Me and my backpack, taking stride,

There will be a room full of noise, strangers all around,

My gentle words, a soothing sound.

"Show your smile, find a friend," I say,

Brave little heart, you find your way.

Sunlight streams, flour flies,
In our kitchen, under bright blue skies.
Tiny hands, dough shapes so sweet,
Stars and bears, hearts beat to beat.
Together we bake, laughter sounds,
In every treat, love abounds.

Morning crisp, leashes to click,

Two pups imagine, their steps so quick.

The sun paints skies in shades so bright,

On quiet streets, we find delight.

Tails wag, a happy song,

In morning light, we all belong.

Thunder roars, screen flickers bright,

On our blanket, we hide from night.

Shadows dance, you snuggle near,

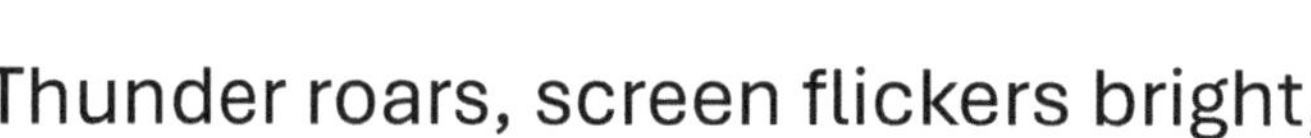

My voice calms, "No monsters here."

Giggles rise, fear takes flight,

Together, we brave the movie night.

Through the glass they drink, and dreams come to light

I ♥ The two enjoying a date with thoughts in sight.

Red curls, perfume's gentle trace,

A mother's heart, a nervous pace.

She left with a smile, she turned to me,

"Have fun," I whispered, I set her free.

BE MINE

Homecoming night, remember it dear,

Your dress shines bright, with joy over fear.

Heels click, smiles wide, lighting the way,

A photo pose, in memories we'll stay.

Proud by your side, my girl so grown,

Under starry lights, your dreams are shown.

Tears like rain, a heart so sore,

In my arms, you're safe, together once more.

No words, just hugs, a storm outside,

In mom's embrace, you can always hide.

Together, quiet, through sorrow we stride,

Love's warm light will be our guide.

Years have flown, you've grown so tall,

In white lace dressed, in love you fall.

Down the aisle, hand in mine,

A radiant bride, truly divine.

Love now shared, a future bright,

With pride, I watch your love take flight.

Twenty-five years, my, how you've grown,

While teaching young children how to hit their tone.

Young voices sing, spirits fly,

Under your lead, notes reach the sky.

Dreams of melody, shared and sung,

A world healed by every note strung.

Two sons I raised, with grace and might,

One flies high, in skies so bright.

The other guards, with steps so sure,

In blue and green, their hearts so pure.

Though worry stings, pride shines clear,

They serve with love, their path so dear.

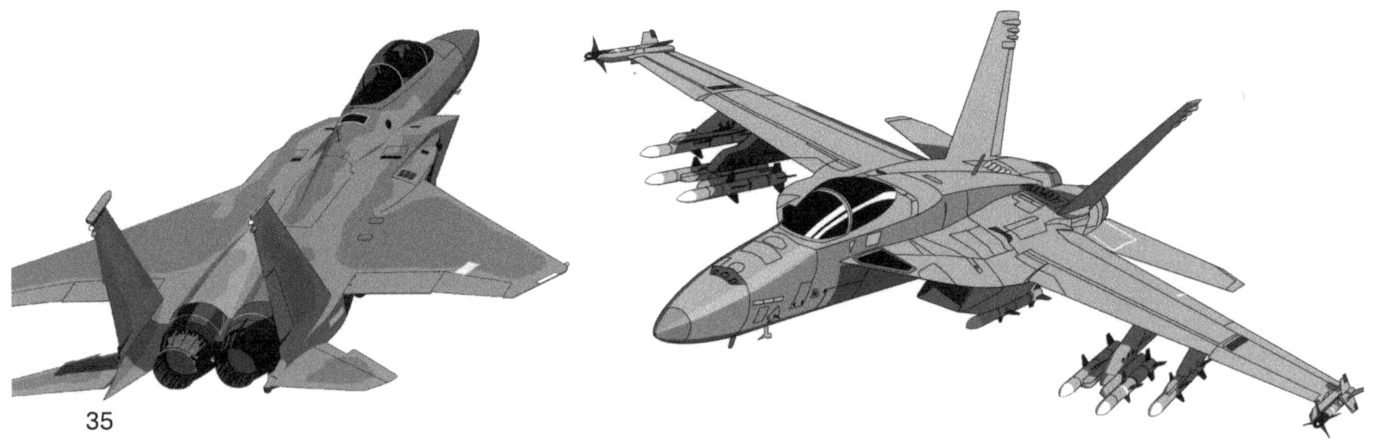

Back to the bench, where dreams once flew,

The setting sun paints shadows anew.

A sigh for years that passed so fast,

In each wrinkle, stories vast.

"Time flies," I whisper, tears might start,

Yet love's warm glow fills my heart.

Door swings wide, laughter so light,

Grandkids' joy, a beautiful sight.

"Grandma! Grandma!" their voices ring,

In my eyes, the memories begin to spring.

Hugs so tight, hearts take flight,

In their laughter, my world is forever bright.

The End!

About the Author

Michael Paladines lives in a suburb outside Chicago. His wife and children have loved being together as a family unit and enjoying spending many hours together. Camping, hiking, and baseball are the hobbies that he enjoys most with his family. He is a professor and teaches health department food safety certification around the Midwest. This is his first book and is eager to tell more stories in the near future.